75 Writing Prompts for Teens

75 Writing Prompts for Teens

Text copyright © 2015 Valerie O'Brien

vobrienwriter@gmail.com

For more about the author, please visit http://www.v-obrien.com

This book is dedicated to all the English teachers in the world. If you've ever struggled in the classroom to get teenagers to write and enjoy the process of writing, trust me, I over stand. Here are some that have worked quite well for me in my six years as an educator. These prompts can be used for quick writes, paragraph work, or 5 paragraph essays. Adapt them to your lessons on writing. I hope this book helps you in some way. Be well.

Prompt #1

Write about a recent current event in your community or the news.
How has this event impacted you and your community?

Prompt #2

Write about what you would do if you won two hundred million dollars in the lottery.

Prompt #3

Tell a story about being cheated on and explain how you would
handle the situation.

Prompt #4

Write an essay on how to set up a social media account. Provide details about the page setup, privacy features, sharing media, etc.

Prompt #5

Write a description of your favorite film or television star. Who is this person? How did this person gain celebrity? Why is this person your favorite?

Prompt #6

Write about how to mend the relationship between two best friends who had a terrible argument.

Prompt #7

Why is social media important to you? Write an essay to explain at least 3 reasons why social media is an important aspect of your life.

Prompt #8

Someone has stolen your friend's cell phone. You know who the
thief is. Write an essay that tells how you plan to resolve this matter.

Prompt #9

If you could have dinner with a celebrity, who would it be? Write an essay that tells who you're having dinner with and be sure to provide details about the outing.

Prompt #10

What's your favorite magazine? Why is it so special to you? Write an essay tells all about your favorite magazine and explain why this one is a favorite.

Prompt #11

Write about the worst fight you've ever witnessed in real-life or in the media. In your essay offer two alternate options for avoiding a fight with someone.

Prompt #12

What's the latest dance move? Write an essay that describes this dance move. Be sure to explain how it's done and how you feel when you do it.

Prompt #13

Write about your favorite shoe or clothing brand. Explain why this particular brand of shoe or clothing is a favorite.

Prompt #14

How do you prefer your hair styled? And where do you like to have your hair done? Why? Write an essay that addresses these questions.

Prompt #15

What kind of car would you like to drive as an adult? Write an essay that tells the make and model of your car choice and be sure to provide some uses for having a car of this type and explain why you think it's one you should own someday.

Prompt #16

Write an essay that tells someone who's never had a cell phone how to set it up and use it in all the ways that you do.

Prompt #17

Why do you think YouTube is popular today? Write an essay that explains its popularity.

Prompt #18

Write an essay to persuade a friend to lend you money. The amount is your decision. Be sure to include a reason why you need this money and how you plan to repay it.

Prompt #19

A new kid at school is being teased about the clothes he or she has on. How would you handle this situation? Write an essay that explains your actions toward resolving this matter.

Prompt #20

Have you ever been to a party and it was the worst party of your entire life? What were your thoughts? How did you deal with this situation? Write an essay in response to these questions and be sure to give details about this awful party.

Prompt #21

You've been accused of being a snitch for telling the truth about cyberbullying on Facebook. Write an essay that tells your thoughts and emotions on the matter.

Prompt #22

Why do you think poverty exists in the world? Write an essay to explain your thoughts on poverty and offer some solutions to ending it.

Prompt #23

Consider a long, hot shower or a good soak in a bubble bath. Which do you prefer? Why? Make a choice. Write an essay that addresses this topic and its questions.

Prompt #24

Some say that bottled water is really plain ole tap water. What do
you think? Do a little research on this topic and then write an essay
that argues your claim. Be sure to offer support of your argument.

Prompt #25

Girls are better than boys are at keeping a secret. How do you feel about this statement? Write an essay that explains which gender is better at keeping a secret and why you believe this is so.

Prompt #26

For a relationship to last there must be mutual trust. Do you believe this statement? Write an essay that gives your opinion on this topic.

Prompt #27

Who makes life better for you? Write an essay that tells who makes life better for you. Be sure to include details of how this person adds to the quality of your life.

Prompt #28

Write an essay that describes your favorite snack foods. Limit your descriptions to 3 snack food items.

Prompt #29

What's your zodiac sign? For this one, conduct a little research on your zodiac sign and determine if the information matches who you really are then write an essay about it.

Prompt #30

Write an essay on all the possible uses for paper and plastic goods such as paper towels, plates, cups, and utensils.

Prompt #31

How do you feel about writing? Does it make you angry or do you
enjoy it? Write an essay that explains your thoughts on writing.

Prompt #32

Why do some teens drop out of high school? Write an essay that explores at least 3 reasons why teens don't finish high school.

Prompt #33

You've been asked to go out with someone who you don't really like. How will you handle this situation?

Prompt #34

Your family has planned a camping trip. But you hate everything about the outdoors. Write an essay to convince your family to allow you to skip this trip and stay home.

Prompt #35

Write an essay that tells how you get a girl or a guy to like you.

Prompt #36

Consider all that you do to unwind, you know, what you do to take a load off. Write an essay that tells how you relax.

Prompt # 37

Write about the best field trip you've ever been on. Why was it so much fun for you?

Prompt #38

Write about a school subject you think is boring. Be sure to explain why it's boring.

Prompt #39

Write about a typical day in your life. Be sure to describe everything that happens in your day.

Prompt #40

Outside you overhear two neighbors arguing, and then they fight in your front yard. How does this incident make you feel? How do you react to the matter?

Prompt #41

Write about one song that you can listen to on repeat because it's just that great. Provide details about the singer and song. You can also explain why this song is one to repeatedly listen to.

Prompt #42

Write an essay that describes what it's like to ride a rollercoaster.

Prompt #43

It's your job to make dinner tonight. What kind of meal will you cook for the family? Write an essay that tells about your plan and preparation of the family dinner.

Prompt #44

Write about your favorite hobby or sport. And if you don't have an interest in either one, then write about a topic you can speak intelligently about.

Prompt #45

Write an essay about 3 skills you must have in order to get a job.

Prompt #46

When listening, girls are better at it than boys. What do you think about this statement? Write an essay that explains who you believe is the better listener.

Prompt #47

Write an essay about your favorite electronic device. Be sure to explain why this one is a favorite.

Prompt #48

Bullies are the worst. Write an essay that tells how you would deal with someone who was bullying you every day at school.

Prompt #49

If you had the chance to skydive, ride in a hot air balloon, or climb
the world's largest mountain, which one would you choose? Write
an essay about your choice and explain your reason why?

Prompt #50

Write an essay that lists and describes everything in your closet.

Prompt #51

When writing an essay, do you prefer to type or write it out? Make a choice and then use this method to write your essay. Be sure to include the reason for your choice.

Prompt #52

How would you describe your handwriting style? How did you learn to write this way? What does your handwriting say about your personality? Write an essay that addresses these questions.

Prompt #53

Describe what a tornado is like. How do you think you'd survive in a tornado storm?

Prompt #54

There's $50,000 dollars in cash at the top of a skyscraper. How are you going to get it? Write an essay that provides elaborate details on how you'd go about getting the money.

Prompt #55

You've been invited to a birthday party, but someone you hate is going to be there. How do you handle this situation? Why?

Prompt #56

Describe the worst food you've ever eaten. What was it like for you? Why do you believe it tasted awful?

Prompt #57

Write an essay that explains four ways to get someone's attention using a non-verbal approach.

Prompt #58

Everyone gets angry. How do you handle anger? Write an essay about what makes you angry and some ways in which you deal with anger.

Prompt #59

How large is your family? Write an essay about your family size and what it's like to be in your family.

Prompt #60

As a kid what was your favorite cartoon to watch? Write an essay that provides details about your favorite cartoon.

Prompt #61

How does your closest friend react to stress in life? Write an essay about this and be sure to include how you help your friend overcome stress.

Prompt #62

How do you deal with a common cold? Do you take any medicine or go visit the doctor for treatment? Write an essay on how you deal with a common cold.

Prompt #63

How would you convince someone who's feeling down and out not to give up in life?

Prompt #64

Mosquitoes are such pesky bugs. How do you guard yourself against a mosquito bite? When bitten by a mosquito, what actions do you take?

Prompt #65

Which brand of hot sauce do you think is the hottest? Write an essay that names the brand of the hot sauce and explain why you believe it's the hottest.

Prompt #66

You've been told that the world will end tonight at midnight. How do you feel about this news? How will you prepare for the world coming to an end?

Prompt #67

Write about the strangest noise you've ever heard.

Prompt #68

Why do you think people wear house shoes? Write an essay that offers 3 reasons why people wear house shoes.

Prompt #69

Do you like juice or soda? Write an essay that includes your choice
of beverage and the reason why you like it.

Prompt #70

How would you deal with a pushy and rude salesperson?

Prompt #71

Write an essay that explains 7-10 slang words. Be sure to avoid usage of profanity in your writing.

Prompt #72

One of your classmates keeps farting for attention. The farts stink. How would you handle this matter?

Prompt #73

When you sleep, do you like to lie on a fluffy or flat pillow? Why?

Prompt #74

When you take pictures either alone or with a group of friends, how do you like to pose? Why?

Prompt #75

When you surf the Internet, which browser do you use? Why?